HABITATS

by Tara Haelle

Published in the United States of America by Cherry Lake Publishing Group
Ann Arbor, Michigan
www.cherrylakepublishing.com

Reading Adviser: Beth Walker Gambro, MS, Ed., Reading Consultant, Yorkville, IL

Photo Credits:
© Nicoleta Ionescu/Shutterstock, (cartoon girl on cover and throughout book), © Ethan Daniels / Shutterstock, (coral reef) cover; © Cassette Bleue/Shutterstock, speech bubbles throughout; © Kurit afshen/Shutterstock, (clownfish), © Allexxandar/Shutterstock (coral) © Crystal Eye Media/Shutterstock (map), page 5;© stockphoto-graf/Shutterstock, pages 6-7; © mc_pongsatorn/Shutterstock (clownfish), © Limolida Design Studio/Shutterstock (orange coral background), page 8; © Try_my_best/Shutterstock (bats in cave), © ATTILA Barsan/Shutterstock (one bat), © Kate Kony/Shutterstock (crab), page 9;© MFiamengo/Shutterstock, page 10; © Daniel Poloha/Shutterstock, (kelp), © elakazal/Shutterstock, (otter), page 11;© Beblack-Dplz/Shutterstock, (pond), © topimages/Shutterstock, (frog), page 12; © zaeonWAVE/Shutterstock, (croc), © Subphoto.com/Shutterstock, (shark), page 13; © Kiri Photography/Shutterstock, (lizard), © Lubo Ivanko/Shutterstock, page 14; © CherylRamalho/Shutterstock, (polar bears), © Steve Boice/Shutterstock, (seals), page 15; © Ricardo Reitmeyer/Shutterstock, (buffaloes), © Travel Stock/Shutterstock, savanna, © Ivan Hoermann/Shutterstock (steppes), pages 16-17;© Reforestation Collection/Shutterstock, (forest), © GUDKOV ANDREY/Shutterstock, (toucan), © Christian Vinces/Shutterstock,(jaguar), © mtayyab554/Shutterstock, (snake), © Milan Zygmunt/Shutterstock, (sloth), page 18; © © Reforestation Collection/Shutterstock, (forest), © mentalmind/Shutterstock, (forest illustration, top), page 19; © Virrage images/Shutterstock, page 20; © VectorMine/Shutterstock, page 21

Produced by bluedooreducation.com for Cherry Lake Publishing

Copyright © 2026 by Cherry Lake Publishing Group

All rights reserved. No part of this book may be reproduced or utilized in any form or by any means without written permission from the publisher.

Library of Congress Cataloging-in-Publication Data has been filed and is available at catalog.loc.gov.

Printed in the United States of America

Note from Publisher: Websites change regularly, and their future contents are outside of our control. Supervise children when conducting any recommended online searches for extended learning opportunities.

TABLE OF CONTENTS

The Perfect Home 4

Habitats 8

Water Habitats 10

Deserts 14

Grasslands 16

Forests 18

Think About It 22
Glossary 23
Find Out More 24
Index 24
About the Author 24

THE PERFECT HOME

Look at the cover of this book.
What do you see?

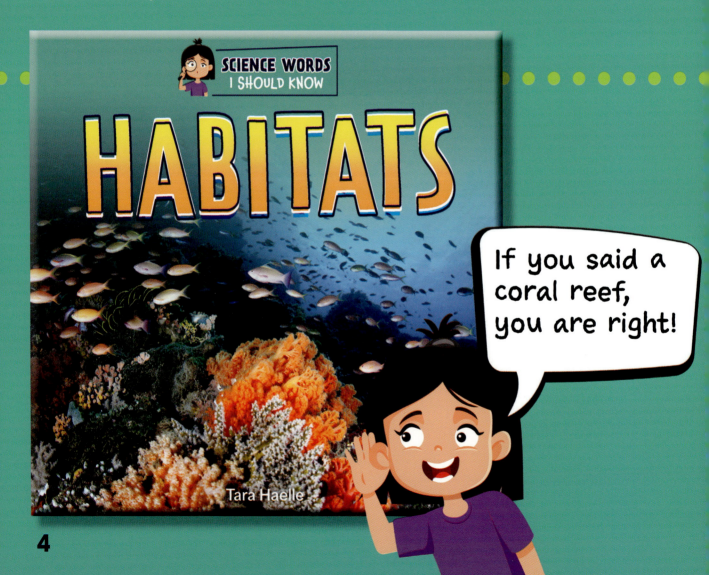

Coral reefs are home to millions of plants and sea animals. One of those animals is the clownfish.

clownfish

The largest coral reef in the world is the Great Barrier Reef. It lies off the coast of Australia.

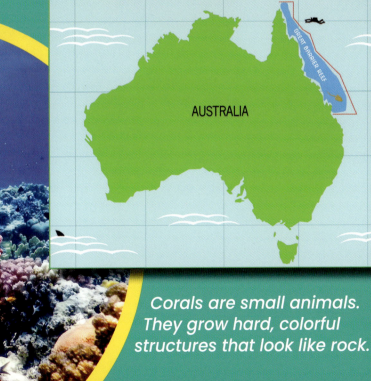

coral

Corals are small animals. They grow hard, colorful structures that look like rock.

Coral reefs are the perfect home for these plants and animals.

This is their **habitat**. It gives them what they need to live and grow.

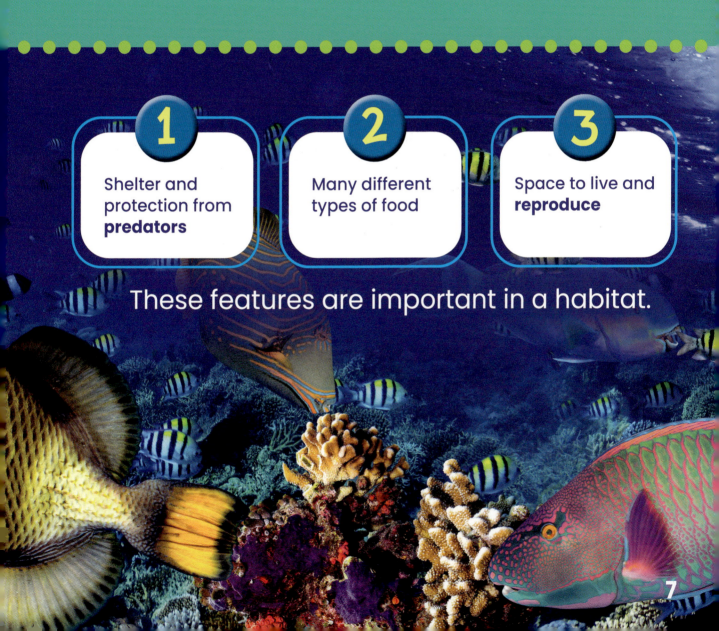

1. Shelter and protection from **predators**
2. Many different types of food
3. Space to live and **reproduce**

These features are important in a habitat.

HABITATS

A habitat is the place where an animal lives. Habitats must have enough space, shelter, food, and water for an animal to **survive**.

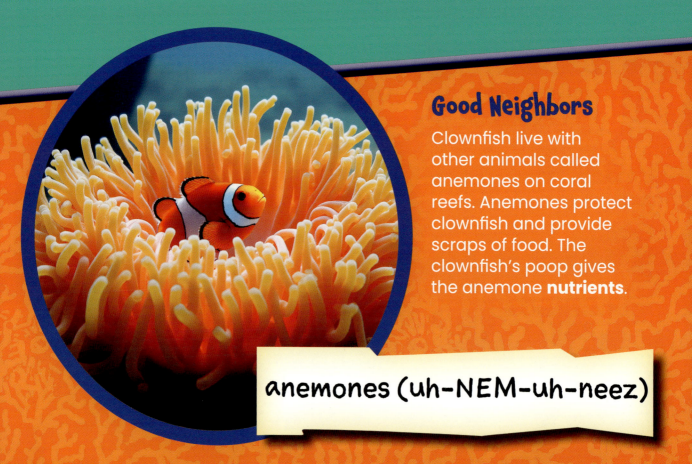

Good Neighbors

Clownfish live with other animals called anemones on coral reefs. Anemones protect clownfish and provide scraps of food. The clownfish's poop gives the anemone **nutrients**.

anemones (uh-NEM-uh-neez)

There are many kinds of habitats.

Bats sleep upside-down?

Bats live in caves. Caves can be safe places for bats to sleep.

Many kinds of crabs like to burrow and hide in the sand.

WATER HABITATS

A coral reef is a marine habitat because it's in the ocean. Two other marine habitats are the ocean floor and a kelp forest.

The dumbo octopus lives deep down on the ocean floor. No sunlight reaches there. It is so dark and cold that there are few predators to hunt the octopus.

1 Can easily hide in the darkness from predators

2 Plenty of hard surfaces, like rocks, for laying their eggs

3 Lots of tiny **prey** above the sand to eat

These features make the ocean floor a good habitat for the octopus.

Kelp are huge brown seaweeds. They grow close to shorelines. They provide shelter from rough ocean currents.

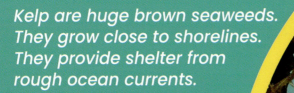

Fish and mammals can hide from predators within the tall kelp stalks.

The safety of a kelp forest makes it a good habitat.

11

Lakes, ponds, rivers, and streams are freshwater habitats. They are home to animals that need fresh water to survive.

Freshwater swamps and marshes allow frogs to spend time on land and in the water.

Freshwater crocodiles live in Australia's lakes and rivers. They are smaller than the saltwater crocodiles that live in Australia's marine waters.

Living in Two Worlds

Most **aquatic** animals only live in saltwater or freshwater. But some can live in both. The bull shark mostly lives in the ocean like other sharks, but it sometimes spends time in freshwater rivers.

bull shark

DESERTS

Deserts are land habitats. They have little water, so they are very dry.

Many kinds of lizards live in the desert. It makes a good home for their needs.

1 Blazing hot sun keeps their bodies warm

2 Lots of insects and plants to eat

These features make the desert a good habitat for some kinds of lizards.

The tundra is a type of desert with extremely cold temperatures.

tundra: TUHN-druh

A polar bear's habitat is the tundra. A polar bear has thick fur to keep warm.

1 Home to lots of seals for polar bears to eat

2 Plenty of space to move around

These features make the tundra a good habitat for polar bears.

15

GRASSLANDS

Grasslands are wide, open stretches of land covered in grasses. Grasslands get more rain than a desert.

The grass provides food for animals to graze. It is a hiding place for predators while they hunt for prey.

prairie

Grasslands in Africa are called savannas. They are called prairies in North America and pampas in South America. In Europe and Asia, grasslands are called steppes.

savanna

steppes

FORESTS

There are different types of forests all over the world. **Tropical** rainforests are hot and wet. They get lots of rain.

Good Neighbors

The Amazon is the largest rainforest in the world. It gets up to 10 feet (3 meters) of rain every year. Toucans, jaguars, anacondas, and sloths all live in the Amazon.

toucan   jaguar   anaconda   sloth

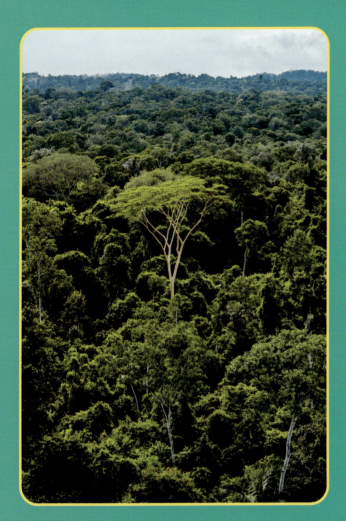
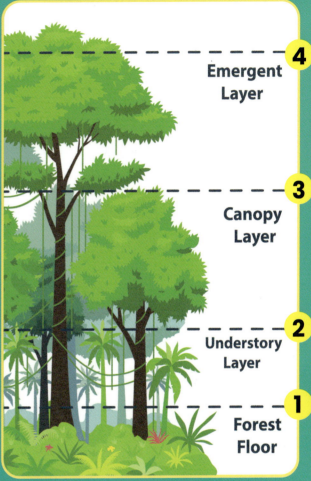

A rainforest has four layers. Each layer is its own habitat. The emergent layer gets the most sunlight. The canopy is home to the most rainforest animals. Small animals like insects, frogs, and geckos live in the two bottom layers.

The main feature of all forest habitats are trees. Trees provide food and shelter for birds and small mammals.

The redwood forests in California have the tallest trees in the world.

Temperate forests change with the seasons. They are home to deer, foxes, squirrels, bears, and birds.

temperate: TEM-pur-it

Some trees in a temperate forest lose their leaves in the fall.

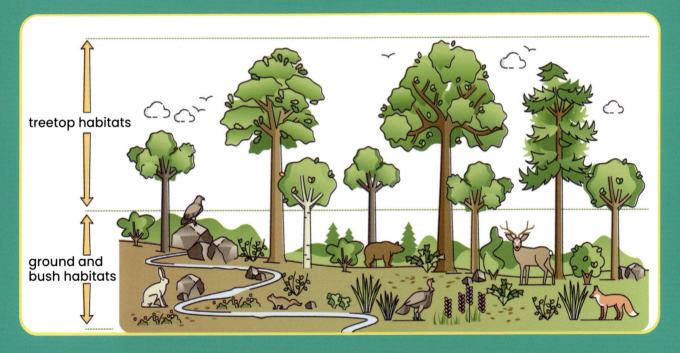

Each habitat around the world is the perfect home for the plants and animals that live there.

THINK ABOUT IT

Using what you have learned in this book, match each sentence to the correct picture.

1 I live where it's dry.

2 My home is in a rainforest.

3 I live in a kelp forest.

4 I roam on prairies in North America.

A.

B.

C.

D.

Answers: 1D 2B 3A 4C

22

GLOSSARY

aquatic (uh-KWAT-ik) animals or plants that live in water

habitat (HAA-buh-tat) the place where a plant or animal usually lives and grows

nutrients (NOO-tree-uhnts) substances that living things need to stay healthy and grow

predators (PRED-uh-turz) animals that hunt and eat other animals

prey (PRAY) animals that are hunted and eaten by other animals

reproduce (ree-pruh-DOOS) to produce offspring

survive (sur-VIEV) to stay alive

tropical (TRAH-pih-kuhl) having to do with the hot, rainy area of the tropics

Find Out More

Books
DK, *Habitats of the World*, London: DK Children, 2023

Pang, Hannah. *Habitats*, Wilson, CT: 360 Degrees, 2024

Websites
Search these online sources with an adult:

Habitats | National Geographic Kids

Habitats | San Diego Zoo Wildlife Alliance

Index

coral reef(s) 4, 5, 6, 8, 10
deserts 14, 15, 16
forest(s) 10, 11, 18, 19, 20, 21
freshwater 12, 13
grasslands 16, 17
predator(s) 7, 10, 11, 16
prey 10, 16
shelter 7, 8, 11, 20
tundra 15

About the Author

Tara Haelle is an author and science journalist who graduated from the University of Texas at Austin. She loves traveling and has backpacked, hiked, train-hopped, sky-dived, spelunked, scuba-dived, and motorbiked through dozens of countries while eating strange insects, trekking to ancient ruins, and swimming with sharks. She lives in Texas with her husband and two sons, four dogs, and 15 pet rats, give or take.